NEXT

. . . . .

BOOKS BY LUCILLE CLIFTON

Poetry

Good Times, 1969
Good News About the Earth, 1972
An Ordinary Woman, 1974
Two-Headed Woman, 1980
Next, 1987

Prose

Generations: A Memoir, 1976

Poetry and Prose

Good Woman:
Poems and A Memoir 1969-1980, 1987

N E X T

. . . .

. . . N E W . P O E M S . . .

L U C I L L E   C L I F T O N

BOA EDITIONS, LTD. ▪ BROCKPORT, NY ▪ 1987

Grateful acknowledgment is made to the editors of the following journals in which some of these poems first appeared: *Confirmation:* "morning mirror" and "my dream about being white"; *Cow in The Road:* "my dream about being white"; *Maryland Poetry Review:* "california lessons"; *Quarry West:* "in white america"; and *Virginia Quarterly Review:* "my dream about time," "my dream about the cows" and "my dream about the second coming."

The following poems appeared in *The American Poetry Review:* "what spells raccoon to me," "this belief," "1. at gettysburg," "1. at nagasaki," "1. at jonestown," "sorrow song," "cruelty. don't talk to me about cruelty," "the lost women," "here is another bone to pick with you," "if our grandchild be a girl," "my dream about the poet," "crazy horse names his daughter," "the message of crazy horse," "the death of thelma sayles" and "shapeshifter poems."

The inscription from "December Day in Honolulu" from *The Past* by Galway Kinnell. Copyright © 1985 by Galway Kinnell. Reprinted by permission of Houghton Mifflin Co.

Manufactured in the United States of America. Except in the case of brief quotations in reviews, no part of this publication may be reproduced or transmitted in any form or by any means without written permission from the publisher. All inquiries should be addressed to: BOA Editions, Ltd., 92 Park Avenue, Brockport, New York 14420.

ISBN 978-0-918526-61-8 (paper)

LC number 87-71304

11 12 13 14   13 12 11 10

Publications by BOA Editions, Ltd., a not-for-profit corporation under section 501(c)(3) of the United States Internal Revenue Service Code, are made possible in part with the assistance of grants from the Literature Program of the New York State Council on the Arts and the Literature Program of the National Endowment for the Arts, a Federal Agency, as well as grants from private foundations, corporations and individuals.

Designed and typeset at Visual Studies Workshop, Rochester, New York.
Manufactured by McNaughton & Gunn, Ann Arbor, MI.
BOA logo by Mirko

State of the Arts

NYSCA

BOA Editions, Ltd.
250 North Goodman Street, Suite 306
Rochester, NY 14607
www.boaeditions.org
A. Poulin Jr., Founder (1938-1996)

ART WORKS.
arts.gov

to fred
see you later alligator

C O N T E N T S

we are all next

or next

singing

This one or that one dies but never the singer. . . one singer falls but the next steps into the empty place and sings. . .

"December Day in Honolulu"
Galway Kinnell

WE ARE ALL NEXT

album
for lucille chan hall

1   it is 1939.
    our mothers are turning our hair
    around rags.
    our mothers
    have filled our shirley temple cups.
    we drink it all.

2   1939 again.
    our shirley temple curls.
    shirley yellow.
    shirley black.
    our colors are fading.

later we had to learn ourselves
back across 2 oceans
into bound feet and nappy hair.

3   1958 and 9.
    we have dropped daughters,
    afrikan and chinese.
    we think
    they will be beautiful.
    we think
    they will become themselves.

4   it is 1985.
    she is.
    she is.
    they are.

      ■

winnie song

a dark wind is blowing
the townships into town.
they have burned your house
winnie mandela
but your house has been on fire
a hundred years.
they have locked your husband
in a cage
and it has made him free.
Mandela. Mandala. Mandala
is the universe. the universe
is burning. a dark wind is blowing
the homelands into home.

.

there

there in the homelands
they are arresting children.
they are beating children
and shooting children.
                  in jo'burg
a woman sits on her veranda.
watching her child.
her child is playing on their lawn.
her man comes home from
arresting children. she smiles.
she offers him a drink.
each morning i practice for
getting that woman.
when her sister calls me sister
i remind myself
she is there.

■

what spells raccoon to me
spells more than just his
bandit's eyes
squinting as his furry woman
hunkers down among the fists
of berries.
oh coon
which gave my grandfather a name
and fed his wife on more than one
occasion
i can no more change my references
than they can theirs.

■

this belief
in the magic of whiteness,
that it is the smooth
pebble in your hand,
that it is the godmother's
best gift,
that it explains,
allows,
assures,
entitles,
that it can sprout singular blossoms
like jack's bean
and singular verandas from which
to watch them rise,
it is a spell
winding round on itself,
grimms' awful fable,
and it turns into capetown and johannesburg
as surely as the beanstalk leads
to the giant's actual country
where jack lies broken at the
meadow's edge
and the land is in ruins,
no magic, no anything.

■

why some people be mad at me sometimes

they ask me to remember
but they want me to remember
their memories
and i keep on remembering
mine.

∎

sorrow song

for the eyes of the children,
the last to melt,
the last to vaporize,
for the lingering
eyes of the children, staring,
the eyes of the children of
buchenwald,
of viet nam and johannesburg,
for the eyes of the children
of nagasaki,
for the eyes of the children
of middle passage,
for cherokee eyes, ethiopian eyes,
russian eyes, american eyes,
for all that remains of the children,
their eyes,
staring at us,   amazed to see
the extraordinary evil in
ordinary men.

.

I. at creation

and i and my body rise
with the dusky beasts
with eve and her brother
to gasp in
the insubstantial air
and evenly begin the long
slide out of paradise.
all life is life.
all clay is kin and kin.

■

I. at gettysburg

if, as they say, this is somehow about myself,
this clash of kin across good farmland, then
why are the ghosts of the brothers and cousins
rising and wailing toward me in their bloody voices,
who are you, nigger woman, who are you?

∎

I.   at nagasaki

in their own order
the things of my world
glisten into ash. i
have done nothing
to deserve this,
only been to the silver birds
what they have made me.
nothing.

.

l.   at jonestown

on a day when i would have believed
anything, i believed that this white man,
stern as my father, neutral in his coupling
as adam, was possibly who he insisted he was.
now he has brought me to the middle of the
jungle of my life. if i have been wrong, again,
father may even this cup in my hand turn against me.

.

them bones
them bones will
rise again
them bones
them bones will
walk again
them bones
them bones will
talk again
now hear
the word of The Lord
            — Traditional

atlantic is a sea of bones,
my bones,
my elegant afrikans
connecting whydah and new york,
a bridge of ivory.

seabed they call it.
in its arms my early mothers sleep.
some women leapt with babies in their arms.
some women wept and threw the babies in.

maternal armies pace the atlantic floor.
i call my name into the roar of surf
and something awful answers.

■

cruelty. don't talk to me about cruelty
or what i am capable of.

when i wanted the roaches dead i wanted them dead
and i killed them. i took a broom to their country

and smashed and sliced without warning
without stopping and i smiled all the time i was doing it.

it was a holocaust of roaches, bodies,
parts of bodies, red all over the ground.

i didn't ask their names.
they had no names worth knowing.

now i watch myself whenever i enter a room.
i never know what i might do.

.

the woman in the camp
cbs news
lebanon
1983

they murdered
27 of my family
counting the babies
in the wombs.
some of the men
spilled seed on the ground.
how much is a thousand
thousand?

i had a child.
i taught her to love.
i should have taught her
to fear.
i have learned about blood
and bullets,
where is the love
in my education?

a woman in this camp
has 1 breast and 2 babies.
a woman in this camp
has breasts like mine.
a woman in this camp
watched the stealing
of her husband.
a woman in this camp
has eyes like mine.

alive
i never thought of other women.
if i am ever alive again
i will hold out my female hands.

∎

the lost women

i need to know their names
those women i would have walked with
jauntily the way men go in groups
swinging their arms, and the ones
those sweating women whom i would have joined
after a hard game to chew the fat
what would we have called each other laughing
joking into our beer? where are my gangs,
my teams, my mislaid sisters?
all the women who could have known me,
where in the world are their names?

■

4 daughters

i am the sieve she strains from
little by little
everyday.

i am the rind
she is discarding.

i am the riddle
she is trying to answer.

something is moving
in the water.
she is the hook.
i am the line.

■

grown daughter

someone is helping me with the onions
who peels in the opposite direction
without tears and promises
different soup. i sit with her
watching her   learning to love her but
who is she   who is she   who

■

here is another bone to pick with you
o mother whose bones i worry for scraps,
nobody warned me about daughters;
how they bewitch you into believing
you have thrown off a pot that is yourself
then one night you creep into their rooms and
their faces have hardened into odd flowers
their voices are choosing in foreign elections and
their legs are open to strange unwieldy men.

■

female

there is an amazon in us.
she is the secret we do not
have to learn.
the strength that opens us
beyond ourselves.
birth is our birthright.
we smile our mysterious smile.

∎

if our grandchild be a girl

i wish for her
fantastic hands,
twelve spiky fingers
symbols of our tribe.
she will do magic
with them,
she will turn personal
abracadabra
remembered from
dahomean women
wearing
extravagant gloves.

■

this is the tale
i keep on telling
trying to get it right;
the feast of women,
the feeding and
being fed.

■

my dream about being white

hey music and
me
only white,
hair a flutter of
fall leaves
circling my perfect
line of a nose,
no lips,
no behind, hey
white me
and i'm wearing
white history
but there's no future
in those clothes
so i take them off and
wake up
dancing.

∎

my dream about the cows

and then i see the cattle of my own town,
rustled already,
prodded by pale cowboys with a foreign smell
into dark pens built to hold them forever,
and then i see a few of them
rib thin and weeping low over
sparse fields and milkless lives but
standing somehow standing,
and then i see how all despair is
thin and weak and personal and
then i see it's only
the dream about the cows.

■

my dream about time

a woman unlike myself is running
down the long hall of a lifeless house
with too many windows which open on
a world she has no language for,
running and running until she reaches
at last the one and only door
which she pulls open to find each wall
is faced with clocks and as she watches
all of the clocks strike
                    NO

.

my dream about falling

a fruitful woman
such as myself
is
falling
notices
she is
an apple
thought
that the blossom
was always
thought
that the tree
was forever
fruitful
a woman
such as
myself.

the fact is the falling.
the dream is the tree.

■

my dream about the second coming

mary is an old woman without shoes.
she doesn't believe it.
not when her belly starts to bubble
and leave the print of a finger where
no man touches.
not when the snow in her hair melts away.
not when the stranger she used to wait for
appears dressed in lights at her
kitchen table.
she is an old woman and
doesn't believe it.

when Something drops onto her toes one night
she calls it a fox
but she feeds it.

∎

my dream about God

He is wearing my grandfather's hat.
He is taller than my last uncle.
when He sits to listen
He leans forward tilting the chair

where His chin cups in my father's hand.
it is swollen and hard from creation.
His fingers drum on His knee
dads stern tattoo.

and who do i dream i am
accepting His attentions?

i am the good daughter who stays at home
singing and sewing.
when i whisper He strains to hear me and
He does whatever i say.

∎

my dream about the poet

a man.
i think it is a man.
sits down with wood.
i think he's holding wood.
he carves.
he is making a world
he says
as his fingers cut citizens
trees and things
which he perceives to be a world
but someone says that is
only a poem.
he laughs.
i think he is laughing.

■

morning mirror

my mother her sad eyes worn as bark
faces me in the mirror. my mother
whose only sin was dying, whose only
enemy was time, frowns in the glass.
once again she has surprised me
in an echo of her life but
my mother refuses to be reflected;
thelma whose only strength was love,
warns away the glint of likeness,
the woman is loosened in the mirror and
thelma lucille begins her day.

■

OR NEXT

. . . .

the death of crazy horse
9/5/1877
age 35

in the hills where the hoop
of the world
bends to the four directions
WakanTanka has shown me
the path men walk is shadow.

i was a boy when i saw it,
that long hairs and grey beards
and myself
must enter the dream to be real.

so i dreamed and i dreamed
and i endured.

i am the final war chief.
never defeated in battle.
Lakotah, remember my name.

now on this walk my bones
and my heart
are warm in the hands of my father.
WakanTanka has shown me the shadows
will break
near the creek called Wounded Knee.

remember my name, Lakotah.
i am the final war chief.
father, my heart,
never defeated in battle,
father, my bones,
never defeated in battle,
leave them at Wounded Knee

and remember our name. Lakotah.
i am released from shadow.
my horse dreams and dances under me
as i enter the actual world.

∎

crazy horse names his daughter

sing the names of the women sing
the power full names of the women sing
White Buffalo Woman who brought the pipe
Black Buffalo Woman and Black Shawl
sing the names of the women sing
the power of name in the women sing
the name i have saved for my daughter sing
her name to the ties and baskets and
the red tailed hawk will take her name and
sing her power to WakanTanka sing
the name of my daughter sing she is
They Are Afraid Of Her.

∎

**crazy horse instructs the young men but in
their grief they forget**

cousins if i be betrayed
paint my body red and
plunge it in fresh water.
i will be restored. if not
my bones will turn to stone
my joints to flint and my spirit
will watch and wait.

it is more than one hundred years.
grandmother earth rolls her shoulders
in despair. her valleys are flooded
fresh with water and blood.
surely the heart of crazy horse must rise
and rebone itself.
to me my tribes.
to me my horses.
to me my medicine.

■

the message of crazy horse

i would sit in the center of the world,
the Black Hills hooped around me and
dream of my dancing horse. my wife

was Black Shawl who gave me the daughter
i called They Are Afraid Of Her.
i was afraid of nothing

except Black Buffalo Woman.
my love for her i wore
instead of feathers. i did not dance

i dreamed. i am dreaming now
across the worlds. my medicine is strong.
my medicine is strong in the Black basket
of these fingers. i come again through this

Black Buffalo woman. hear me;
the hoop of the world is breaking.
fire burns in the four directions.
the dreamers are running away from the hills.
i have seen it. i am crazy horse.

■

the death of thelma sayles
2/13/59
age 44

i leave no tracks so my live loves
can't follow. at the river
most turn back, their souls shivering,
but my little girl stands alone on the bank
and watches. i pull my heart out of my pocket
and throw it. i smile as she catches all
she'll ever catch and heads for home
and her children. mothering
has made it strong, i whisper in her ear
along the leaves.

 ■

lives

to lu in answer to her question

you have been a fisherman,
simple and poor. you
struggled all your days and
even at the end you fought
and did not win. your son
was swimming. fearing
for his life you
rushed toward him. and drowned.

once a doctor, bitter,
born in a cold climate,
you turned your scalpel
on the world and cut your way
to the hangman.

humans who speak of royal lives
amuse Them. you have heard of course
of the splendid court of sheba;
you were then. you were not there.

■

the message of thelma sayles

baby, my only husband turned away.
for twenty years my door was open.
nobody ever came.

the first fit broke my bed.
i woke from ecstasy to ask
what blood is this? am i the bride of Christ?
my bitten tongue was swollen for three days.

i thrashed and rolled from fit to death.
you are my only daughter.

when you lie awake in the evenings
counting your birthdays
turn the blood that clots on your tongue
into poems. poems.

∎

the death of joanne c.
11/30/82
aged 21

i am the battleground that
shrieks like a girl.
to myself i call myself
gettysburg. laughing,
twisting the i.v.,
laughing or crying, i can't tell
which anymore,
i host the furious battling of
a suicidal body and
a murderous cure.

.

enter my mother
wearing a peaked hat.
her cape billows,
her broom sweeps the nurses away,
she is flying, the witch of the ward, my mother
pulls me up by the scruff of the spine
incanting   Live   Live   Live!

■

leukemia as white rabbit

running always running murmuring
she will be furious   she will be
furious, following a great
cabbage of a watch that tells only
terminal time, down deep into a
rabbit hole of diagnosticians shouting
off with her hair   off with her skin and
i am   i am   i am   furious.

.

incantation
overheard in hospital

pluck the hairs
from the head
of a virgin.
sweep them into the hall.
take a needle
thin as a lash,
puncture the doorway
to her blood.
here is the magic word:
cancer.
cancer.
repeat it, she will
become her own ghost.
repeat it, she will
follow you, she will
do whatever you say.

■

chemotherapy

my hair is pain.
my mouth is a cave of cries.
my room is filled with white coats
shaped like God.
they are moving their fingers along
their stethoscopes.
they are testing their chemical faith.
chemicals   chemicals   oh mother mary
where is your living child?

she won't ever forgive me,
the willful woman,
for not becoming a pine box
of wrinkled dust according to plan.
i can hear her repeating my dates:
1962 to 1982 or 3. mother
forgive me, mother believe
i am trying to make old bones.

.

the one in the next bed is dying.
mother we are all next. or next.

■

leukemia as dream/ritual

it is night in my room.
the woman beside me is dying.
a small girl stands
at the foot of my bed.
she is crying and carrying wine
and a wafer.
her name is the name i would have given
the daughter i would have liked to have had.
she grieves for herself and
not for the woman.
she mourns the future and
not the past.
she offers me her small communion.
i roll the wafer and wine on my tongue.
i accept my body. i accept my blood.
eat she whispers. drink and eat.

■

the message of jo

my body is a war
nobody is winning.
my birthdays are tired.
my blood is a white flag,
waving.
surrender,
my darling mother,
death is life.

■

chorus: lucille

something is growing in the strong man.
it is blooming, they say, but not a flower.
he has planted so much in me. so much.
i am not willing, gardener, to give you up to this.

.

64

the death of fred clifton
11/10/84
age 49

i seemed to be drawn
to the center of myself
leaving the edges of me
in the hands of my wife
and i saw with the most amazing
clarity
so that i had not eyes but
sight,
and, rising and turning
through my skin,
there was all around not the
shapes of things
but oh, at last, the things
themselves.

■

"i'm going back to my true identity"
fjc 11/84

i was ready to return
to my rightful name.
i saw it hovering near
in blazoned script
and, passing through fire,
i claimed it. here
is a box of stars
for my living wife.
tell her to scatter them
pronouncing no name.
tell her there is no deathless name
a body can pronounce.

∎

my wife

wakes up, having forgotten.
my closet door gapes wide,
an idiot mouth, and inside
all of the teeth are missing.
she closes her eyes and weeps
toward my space in the bed, "Darling,
something has stolen your wonderful
shirts and ties."

■

the message of fred clifton

i rise up from the dead before you
a nimbus of dark light
to say that the only mercy
is memory,
to say that the only hell
is regret.

∎

SINGING

■ ■ ■ ■ ■ ■ ■

one singer falls but the next steps into the empty place and sings...

"December Day in Honolulu"
Galway Kinnell

in white america

1   i come to read them poems

i come to read them poems,
a fancy trick i do
like juggling with balls of light.
i stand, a dark spinner,
in the grange hall,
in the library, in the
smaller conference room,
and toss and catch as if by magic,
my eyes bright, my mouth smiling,
my singed hands burning.

2   the history

1800's in this town
fourteen longhouses were destroyed
by not these people here.
not these people
burned the crops and chopped down
all the peach trees.
not these people. these people
preserve peaches, even now.

3   the tour

"this was a female school.
my mother's mother graduated
second in her class.
they were taught embroidery,
and chenille and filigree,
ladies' learning. yes,
we have a liberal history here."
smiling she pats my darky hand.

4   *the hall*

in this hall
dark women
scrubbed the aisles
between the pews
on their knees.
they could not rise
to worship.
in this hall
dark women
my sisters and mothers

though i speak with the tongues
of men and of angels and
have not charity . . .

in this hall
dark women,
my sisters and mothers,
i stand
and let the church say
let the church say
let the church say
AMEN.

5   *the reading*

i look into none of my faces
and do the best i can.
the human hair between us
stretches but does not break.
i slide myself along it and
love them, love them all.

6   *it is late*

it is late
in white america.
i stand
in the light of the
7-11
looking out toward
the church
and for a moment only
i feel the reverberation
of myself
in white america
a black cat
in the belfry
hanging
and
ringing.

■

shapeshifter poems

1

the legend is whispered
in the women's tent
how the moon when she rises
full
follows some men into themselves
and changes them there
the season is short
but dreadful   shapeshifters
they wear strange hands
they walk through the houses
at night   their daughters
do not know them

2

who is there to protect her
from the hands of the father
not the windows which see and
say nothing   not the moon
that awful eye   not the woman
she will become with her
scarred tongue   who   who   who   the owl
laments into the evening   who
will protect her   this   prettylittlegirl

3

if the little girl lies
still enough
shut enough
hard enough
shapeshifter may not
walk tonight
the full moon may not
find him here
the hair on him
bristling
rising
up

4

the poem at the end of the world
is the poem the little girl breathes
into her pillow   the one
she cannot tell   the one
there is no one to hear   this poem
is a political poem   is a war poem   is a
universal poem but is not about
these things   this poem
is about one human heart   this poem
is the poem at the end of the world

■

california lessons

1   geography

over there is asia
watching from the water
astounded as siddhartha.
over there, asia,
waiting in the water
for what is surely turning
on the wheel. here
is california
swinging from the edge
of the darkening of america
and over there, sitting,
patient as gautama
enlightened, in the water,
is asia.

2   history

guard your language

what bird remembers
the songs
the miwok sang?

guard your life

pomo
shasta
esalen

peoples
not places

3   *botany*

"all common figs
can produce fertile seeds
if the flowers
are pollinated."

in concord
in 1985
a black man
was hung
from a fig tree.

"the fruit
is dark
and sweet."

4 semantics

in 1942
almost all
the japanese
were concentrated
into camps.
intern ment
but no doctor came.

5 metaphysics

question: what is karma?

answer: there is a wheel
              and it is turning.

■

about the author

Lucille Clifton was born in Depew, New York, and educated at the State University of New York at Fredonia and Howard University. She has taught at Coppin State College, Goucher College, and the American University in Washington, D.C. Her other teaching experiences have included appointments as Elliston Poet at the University of Cincinnati, Jenny Moore Visiting Lecturer in Creative Writing at George Washington University, and Woodrow Wilson Scholar at Fisk University, Trinity College and other universities. She currently teaches at the University of California at Santa Cruz. Clifton's awards and distinctions as a poet and fiction writer include The University of Massachusetts Press' Juniper Prize for poetry, a nomination for the Pulitzer Prize in poetry, an Emmy Award from the American Academy of Television Arts and Sciences, creative writing fellowships from the National Endowment for the Arts and Poet Laureate of the State of Maryland.

BOA EDITIONS, LTD.
AMERICAN POETS CONTINUUM SERIES